The unveiling of the Prince Albert statue at Albert Pier, St Peter Port, in 1863. Cast in bronze, it stood on a pedestal of Cornish granite and commemorated the visit of Queen Victoria and the Prince Consort in 1846. It remained unscathed throughout the Second World War, possibly because of the prince's German birth. This engraving, by an unknown artist, is far from realistic – it was pouring with rain at the time of the ceremony.

GUERNSEY
Pictures from the Past

High Street on a misty morning in the 1950s.

GUERNSEY
Pictures from the Past

Carel Toms

Phillimore

1991

Published by
PHILLIMORE & CO. LTD.,
Shopwyke Hall, Chichester, Sussex

ISBN 0 85033 783 6

Printed and bound in Great Britain by
BIDDLES LTD.,
Guildford, Surrey

This volume is dedicated to Victor Coysh, who spent so many happy years of his life writing newspaper articles, detailed historical studies, books on the Bailiwick of Guernsey and particularly volumes like the present one. His knowledge of the islands is profound, and in compiling this book I have sought his help, which he has gladly given. I am also grateful to him for having read the manuscript and corrected errors.

List of Illustrations

Frontispiece: High Street in the 1950s

Acknowledgements

Islanders have once again been most co-operative in loaning their photographs for publication as well as helping to identify the subjects and people in them. The author is grateful to the following, as well as numerous others who have taken an interest in keeping their pictures from the past as reminders of how the Bailiwick of Guernsey has changed: Victor Coysh, John and Isobel Davidson, B. G. Blampied, Ernest De Garis, Mrs. A. Moullin, Peter Brehaut, Philip Le B. Nicholson, M. P. Joyner, Roger Finch, Norman Wilkinson, Royal Guernsey Agricultural and Horticultural Society, Guernsey Post Office, A. J. Maunder, B. J. Girard, R. O. Falla, O.B.E., Mrs. Jean Dilcock, Kevin Le Scelleur, Graham Lawson, Guernsey Press Co. Ltd., Ancient Monuments Committee, Priaulx Library, Guille-Allès Library, Simon Masterton, Rex Bragg, The Greffe Office, Sark, J. H. Lenfestey, Peter Girard, Gresham Barber, John G. Sherwill and Roger Martin.

Thanks are also due to Roger Finch for much of the information on early photographers contained in the introduction, as well as the comprehensive list of photographers which he compiled over many years of research in the Guille-Allès and Priaulx libraries.

Introduction

Following the invention of photography during the first half of the 19th century, the art of producing visible images was quickly acquired by a large number of people who set themselves up as professional photographers with their own studios. In Guernsey, the first is thought to have been Mr. Peers of 18 Berthelot Street, St Peter Port, who opened a studio in April 1842. He was followed a year later by A. Barber, who also set up business in Berthelot Street in May 1843.

This was just four years after Louis Jacques Mande Daguerre (1784-1851) had invented his process of using sensitised copper plates in 1839. A. Barber produced daguerreotypes at his studio in Berthelot Street from 1843 onwards, which were no larger than 2¼ in. by 1¾ in. As with many early photographers who operated in the island, Barber stayed only for the summer season, when he would advertise his services in the local newspapers.

When William Henry Fox Talbot (1800-77) began his paper negative process and calotypes began to appear in the 1850s, the system was used in Guernsey by Captain

The French photographer Arsène Garnier was in business at 1 Havilland Street in 1848. Among his sitters was Victor Hugo. In 1850 he worked from 18 Berthelot Street, and later moved to 3 St James' Street, where he remained. He specialised in tinted photographs and had royal appointments to Queen Victoria, the French emperor and the king of the Belgians.

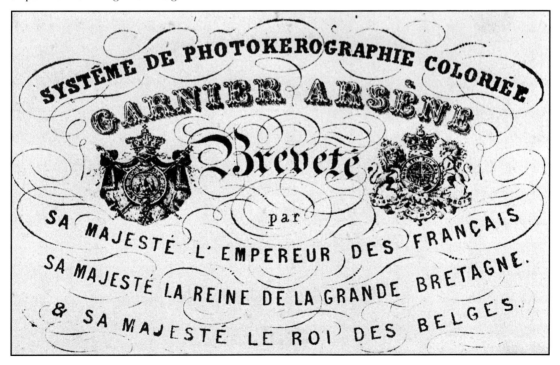

One of the few women to run a photographic studio was Miss Cumber, who operated from 3 Pollet from the mid-1860s until the mid-1880s.

E. Amet of Havelet. He is mentioned in an almanack of 1861, and one of his calotypes, taken in about 1850, is in the Priaulx Library.

Although cameras were starting to be mass produced by about 1884, they were cumbersome and usually made from solid mahogany. Next came a mixture of wood and steel, and when the lightweight box and folding cameras arrived photography entered a new and popular phase.

Professionals, however, held the field until about the time of the First World War. They included photographers such as James Burnside, who operated at 5 Pollet in the late 19th century, before the establishment was taken over by T. A. Grut, who had first worked from 2 Victoria Crescent between 1879 and 1894. Norman Grut followed at the Pollet, and he was succeeded by his son, Alan N. Grut, whose son, Dave, now runs the business. One of the few professional women photographers operating during the 19th century was Miss Cumber of H. J. Cumber, a chemist who founded a business at 3 Pollet in 1818. Miss Cumber had a studio there from the mid-1860s until the mid-1880s. This is now part of Grut's.

Excellent sharp pictures were produced in these studios. The photographs were both shot and printed by daylight. They were printed in sepia on very thin paper and mounted on thick card, often with bevelled gold edges. They came in cabinet size (usually 6 in. by 4 in.) or as *cartes de visite* (usually 4 in. by 2½ in.).

The photographer usually made the best possible use of the space below his client's photograph to advertise himself. James Burnside, for example, chose Old English type printed in gold, and mentioned that he had received a bronze medal for his work in 1889. B. Collenette, who was well known for his landscapes, was at 15 Smith Street in 1878 and moved to 7 Union Street in 1894. He went further than James Burnside and printed a device in gold with the words *Toujours Pret* ('Always Ready'), with his name printed in large script. T. A Grut had a cheaper version, which was without a seal. His name was printed in silver script and the edges were neither bevelled or silvered. A *carte de visite* by R. Dumaresq, whose studio was at 3 St James' Street in the 1890s, bore the information: 'negatives kept. Copies or enlargements can always be had'.

Photographers such as T. Bramley and F. W. Guérin ventured well beyond their studios to record events which were taking place around the island. They sought out work or were commissioned to photograph large groups or special events. Much of their work was purely speculative.

In the latter part of the 19th century, with the invention of the half-tone process, came the era of the press photographer. This phase did not reach the island until the early part of the 20th century, when special darkroom equipment was installed by the Guernsey Press Company. A new breed of photographer emerged: men who rushed to accidents and disasters as well as to social and sporting events. They went on assignments at the behest of editors hungry for news. Some of them carried notebooks as well as cameras, thus performing a dual role. A few press photographers of the past who spring to mind are Jack Le Pavoux, William Vaudin, Charles H. Toms, Ronald Mauger, Charles H. Coker, Kenneth McLeod and Eric Sirett.

Carte de Visite.

Bibliography

Brett, C. E. B., *Buildings in the Town and Parish of St Peter Port*
Gurney, David, *The Channel Islands Sub Post Offices and their Post Marks*
Masterton, Simon, *A Century of Shipping*
McCormack, John, *The Guernsey House*
Moore, R. D., *Methodism in the Channel Islands*

THE SEA

1. St Sampson's Harbour, completed in 1843, is very quiet today. However, it was used by sailing ships well into this century, when pilots had to manoeuvre vessels into crowded berths such as this one on the north side of the harbour.

2. S.S. *Diana* leaving St Peter Port about 1885. The vessel was built for the London and South West Railway Company and was the first screw-propelled ship to be built for the Channel Islands Service, being launched in 1876. In 1885 she went aground off Cap de la Hague, and two days later slid off the rocks and sank.

3. The crew of a Great Western Railway ship at St Peter Port. Some are wearing guernseys with the emblem 'Royal Mail G.W.R.' and an anchor motif. Included in the photograph are the ship's cook and a steward, surrounded by empty tomato baskets being returned to the island. The G.W.R. operated from Weymouth. Railway company shipping services to and from the U.K. started in 1848.

4. The 173-ton paddle steamer *Sir Francis Drake* arrived in Guernsey from Plymouth on 6 January 1900, with two divers on board to help salvage the Great Western Railway ship *Ibex*. The day before, the *Ibex* had hit the Platte Fougère rocks north of Guernsey with the loss of two lives. She was later salvaged and towed to Birkenhead for total rebuilding. The *Sir Francis Drake* had been employed as a tender at Plymouth and in 1908 was renamed the *Helper*. She was purchased by the Alderney Steam Packet Company and ran excursions from Guernsey to Sark, and occasionally to Alderney. In 1927 she was badly damaged in Sark's Creux Harbour, and was replaced by the S.S. *Riduna*.

5. This photograph was taken between 1881 and 1886. The lifeboat house, near the centre, was built in 1881, when the slipway from which the pulling lifeboats were launched had not yet been completed. In 1886 the present-day pond was built on the site of the marquee, to compensate for the loss of the pond at St Julian's when the pier was built there. It became known as 'Queen Victoria's Model Yacht Pond' in honour of the 1897 jubilee.

6. The *Arthur Lionel* (1912-29) was the last pulling lifeboat to be stationed by the R.N.L.I. in Guernsey and was donated by Sir Thomas Tobin of County Cork at a cost of £1,000. She was 35 ft. in length with a beam of 10 ft., and was equipped with 10 oars. John N. Gillman was the cox, and David Luscombe second cox.

7. A very early photograph showing a Les Hanois relief vessel at Portelet, Pleinmont, from where the boat set out. It was customary for a crew to be recruited from among the local fishermen, whose knowledge of rocks and tides in this area was intimate. On board the vessel are barrels in which water was carried to the rock.

8. Two generations of the Le Couteur family were responsible for revictualling Les Hanois Lighthouse when it was manned by keepers whose families lived at Trinity House Cottages, Pleinmont. George Le Couteur Senior (on the left with the cigar) is assisting with the winching up of sacks of coal to a door in the tower. Forty half-hundredweight sacks was the usual amount, as well as 40 wooden kegs of fresh water, each of which had to be craned up and tipped into a storage well. Paraffin, methylated spirit and spare gas mantles were also brought to the rock before electrification.

9. Standing at the base of Les Hanois Lighthouse is a Trinity House keeper, George Le Couteur Junior, and members of his 'crew' who made regular maintenance trips to the lighthouse by sea before a helipad was installed. On the far right is Mr. Guy Blampied, representing the Women's Royal Voluntary Service, who regularly sent comforts to the keepers, especially at Christmas.

10.-13.   For many years mariners had been urging the States of Guernsey to erect a beacon on the Roustel Rock, a reef which lies in mid-channel east of Bordeaux Harbour. A black buoy marked the reef but matters came to a head when, on 10 March 1923, the Southern Railway cargo ship *Ulrica* hit the rock and limped into St Peter Port with holds flooded. Very quickly, tenders were sought to erect a concrete tower and light on the reef. Local contractors, George Le M. Le Couteur, carried out the work at a cost of £2,544.

10.   This photograph shows George Le Couteur Senior supervising the building of Roustel Beacon shortly after work started.

11.   An early stage in construction: supplies of sand, cement and siftings were ferried to the rock in small boats.

12. Well on the way to completion, George Le Couteur
Junior views the work in progress.

13. The almost completed beacon, one of several lighted
towers in this treacherous channel between Guernsey
and Herm.

14. A section of the States Works Department occasionally takes to the sea to maintain the many beacons off Guernsey and Herm which mark hazardous rocks. This is Longue Pierre Rock, off St Martin's Point.

15. The former Brixham trawler *Espero*, which had been used in the filming of Victor Hugo's *Toilers of the Sea* in 1936, sank in the Careening Hard in 1937. She was later sold by auction for £20 to the Rev. G. A. Tait, whose idea was to enable the vessel to be used by the island's Sea Scouts. The plan never materialised.

16.   In October 1926, pilot Emile Noyon purchased the schooner *Bessie*, which was lying partly dismantled at South Side, St Sampson's. Intending to beach the ship at Bordeaux and break her up, he began to tow her there, but she struck a rock off Houmet Benest near Bordeaux. Attempts to move her failed and she was broken up where she lay. This photograph was taken a year later. The ship's figurehead was for many years in a cottage garden at Cognon Road, North Side, Vale.

17.   In 1952 the Guernsey-owned ship S.S. *Fermain* went aground near the Black Rock, North Side, Vale, while en route from Swansea with 1,300 tons of coal. The lifeboat *Queen Victoria* and the pilot boat *Dolphin* took off the master and crew of thirteen. Early in 1953 Guernsey Contractors Ltd. and John Upman Ltd. bought the wreck, opened the ship's side and salvaged the coal, which was badly needed to heat the island's glasshouses. The vessel was later broken up where she lay.

18. Although it is no longer possible to hold regattas in St Peter Port Harbour, they were almost annual events in the early part of the century, until the last war. These half-decked gaff-rigged boats were racing at the mouth of the harbour on 1 August 1907.

19. The first speedboat service to operate to Herm opened on 27 June 1948. The boat, here seen leaving an almost empty Albert Dock, was run by Alderney-born Bonnie Newton, a wartime hero who took part in a commando raid on Les Casquets Lighthouse.

20. Sand yachting arrived in Guernsey in 1952, and three islanders were involved in building these 'boats on wheels' which flew along the sands at Vazon Bay. John Davidson, Roy Mallet and Lionel Frampton built the first such boats from scrap wood and used inflated wheelbarrow wheels. The sport, however, never really took off.

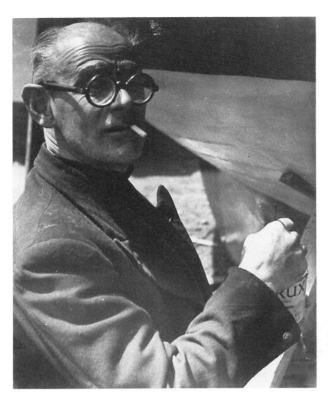

21. (*Left*) In 1926 Arthur J. Barber of Beauregard, St Peter Port, built a 21½-ft. yacht which he named *Cockleshell*. The yacht survived the Occupation, suffering only some shrapnel 'wounds' from a British bomb. It is still in commission and winning races, sailed by Jonathon Sherwill. 'A. J.', as Mr. Barber was known, was a dental surgeon with a passionate love of the sea. He is seen here painting *Cockleshell*, which has always been red.

22. (*Below*) This beautiful scale model of the *Cockleshell* was made by the late John Sherwill, son of a former bailiff of Guernsey, Sir Ambrose J. Sherwill.

23. The *Ormer* was one of several boats built by A. J. Barber. Because of the severe post-war wood shortage, it was made of the wood from two old boats. This picture shows Mr. Barber's son, Max (astern), and his family on an outing between the islands. *Ormer* is still in use and is moored in the Bordeaux area.

24.   In 1950 the Guernsey Yacht Yard at North Side was run by Captain Mervyn Wood. As well as repairing yachts and other vessels he built the popular Weymouth Falcon Class yacht. Among the vessels on the slip is former Brixham trawler, *Smiling Morn*. The yard was later acquired by John Upham Ltd. and became a ship survey and repair centre. It is now operated by Marine and General Engineers Ltd., and was transformed to accommodate ships and hydrofoils.

PLACES

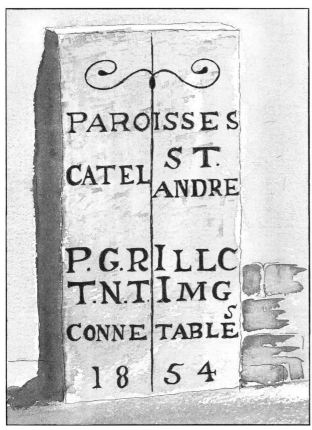

25. This boundary stone between the parishes of the Câtel (Castel) and St André (St Andrew's) is at the junction of Rue de la Cache and Rue des Varendes.

26. This parish boundary stone stands on the south side of the Route des Laurens and Route de la Palloterie.

27. On 11 December 1911 part of the high wall adjacent to what is known as the Cat's Ladder, linking Cordier Hill with Vauvert, collapsed. It brought down tons of rubble into the road and caused chaos to the horse and cart traffic flow. Thomas Bramley was there to record the event with his camera. In February 1987 the same wall fell down, again causing traffic problems. It was three-and-a-half years before the Cat's Ladder was re-opened to the public.

28. The only building in this photograph still recognisable is the Picquet House, once a guard house. The buildings on the left, which stood in front of the town church, were demolished in 1914. The foot of Fountain Street narrowed here, where it was joined by Cornet Street. Following the demolitions, a slip road was constructed up to Cornet Street with steps down into Fountain Street. In the wall is a barometer kept by the R.N.L.I., which was last attended to in June 1940. Hoardings were once familiar features in various parts of the island.

29. The medieval No. 12 Le Pollet, St Peter Port, became a public house known as *Le Briseur's*, having been run for many years by a lady of that name. It was sold for £5,200 in 1951 to make way for an extension to a furniture store.

30. The first Methodist church in the Channel Islands was opened in 1789 at Rue Le Marchant, St Peter Port. The Truchot Street chapel, shown in this 1933 photograph, dated from the late 19th century and was one of the last to be built. It was demolished during the 1980s, along with most of the rest of the street, to make way for merchant banks. Below the chapel can be seen one of the last of the ancient wine vaults, which has also vanished.

31. This 17th-century house, 'Luarca', stands beside the present coast road at Pulias, St Sampson's, once a very isolated area. No longer thatched, half of it was demolished when the 19th-century house alongside it was built.

32. In 1990 the last of the original hand-operated harbour cranes with wooden jibs was removed from the north side of St Sampson's Harbour, where it had stood since 1843. After refurbishment it was placed in the Maritime Museum, Castle Cornet. The modern crane (left) has also been removed and the site of the buildings has been re-developed. On the right were the premises of William Bird, the coal merchant. Marmaduke Hunkin occupied the building in the centre, which was a sailmaker's loft.

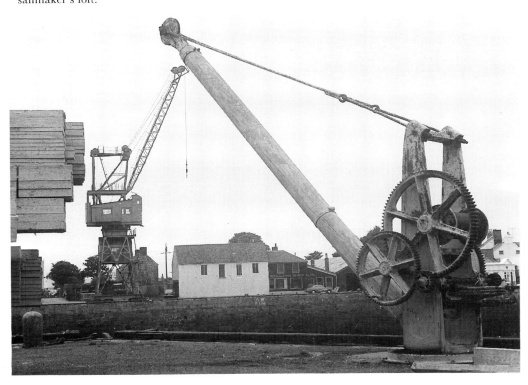

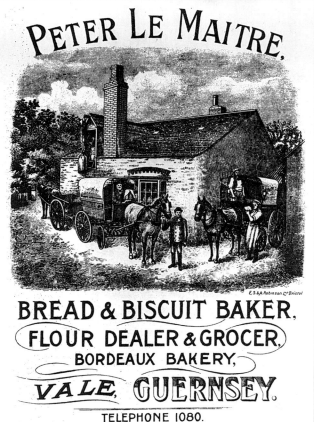

PETER LE MAITRE,

BREAD & BISCUIT BAKER,
FLOUR DEALER & GROCER,
BORDEAUX BAKERY,
VALE, GUERNSEY.

TELEPHONE 1080.

33. Bordeaux House in Rue du Havre, Bordeaux, Vale, is one of the island's most ancient dwellings. It appears on the 1787 Duke of Richmond Survey. This early photograph shows it thatched but with stucco covering the front. It was once owned by Peter Le Maitre, who operated a bakery at the rear.

34. Peter Le Maitre was a bread and biscuit maker who had a bakery at Bordeaux. The Le Maitre brothers were famous for their Guernsey Gâche cake, of which they supplied almost two tons during the coronation of King Edward VII. At the 1937 North Show and Battle of Flowers they sold 11 cwt.

35. Trafalgar House is an attractive house built of blue dressed granite at North Side, Vale. Mr. J. Ogier built it with the intention of using it as a public house. It was later run as a shop, becoming a café in the 1950s.

36. Bordeaux Harbour was a tranquil place during the last century with just a few two-masted fishing boats. Beyond is the Vale castle, a medieval defence work which guarded the north-east coast of Guernsey when it was two islands divided by the Braye du Valle waterway. Over the years the castle was modernised and garrisoned, being occupied last by the Germans, who moved out in 1945. All its outworks and barracks have now disappeared.

37. The outworks at the Vale Castle stood beside the present-day arched entrance.

38. 'Wisteria', King's Mills, Castel, was built between 1584 and 1634. When constructed there were no buildings between it and the sea. It was the home of Nicholson Le Beir, a major in the North Regiment of the Royal Guernsey Militia.

39. Extending from the corner of Rue du Presbytère and along Le Rohais de Haut once stood a row of cottages. In 1914 they were demolished to make way for a new entrance to the Castel parish church and also to provide an extension to the cemetery.

40. Blanchelande College, St Martin's, soon after it was built in the 1930s. The circular corrugated iron huts in the Moulin Huet valley, above which stands the college, were occupied by a local family and have long since vanished. Several orders of sisters have successfully run the college and farm. The present incumbents are the Sisters of Our Lady of Mercy.

41. These two houses – Hinton and Bransgore – were once owned by the Tostevin family, who ran a garage and cycle business at La Grande Rue, St Martin's. They were demolished in 1988 to make way for a garage.

42a. & b. The small island of Houmet Paradis lies off the east coast of Guernsey, just north of Petils Bay. There was once a small farmhouse there; the photograph above shows part of its oven in 1914. Within living memory a couple and their daughter lived on Houmet Paradis and kept a cow which they walked across to the mainland at low tide to graze. The island (*below*) is in the care of the National Trust of Guernsey.

43-45. Some mystery will probably always surround the origin of these pottery ridge tiles. Two are in Guernsey and one adorns a house in Alderney. There are parallels in the West Country but they are most likely to have come from Normandy where similar tiles were made in the Cotentin.

43. (*Top left*) Ridge tile at La Grande Rue, St Martin's.

44. (*Top right*) This tile at the slaughter house is well-worn and has lost its head. Although the slaughter house was built in 1887, the tile may have come from an older building.

45. (*Below left*) This tile at 'Les Chevaliers', Alderney, is one of four brought from France by the Tourgis family. Three vanished during the Occupation.

46. (*Right*) Among the odd details on the ends of the roof ridges of the Lower Vegetable Market, completed in 1879, are two large bronze-leaved tobacco plants. These finials, one of which is shown here, commemorate the tax on tobacco imposed by the States to help finance the building's construction.

PEOPLE

47.   The wedding of Mr. and Mrs. Frank de M. Lainé took place at St Andrew's Church on 7 August 1913. From left to right are Mr. and Mrs. Thomas Mauger Bichard (the bride's parents), Mr. and Mrs. Lainé (the bridegroom and bride), Mr. Eustace Lainé (best man), Mr. and Mrs. E. T. Lainé (the bridegroom's father and mother), Miss Eva Duquemin and Miss Dorothy Lainé (bridesmaids). The photographer was W. J. Woodwards of St Peter Port.

48.   The family of Eugene Thomas Lainé at their home 'Les Bourgs', St Andrew's, photographed *c*.1914. In the back row are the four boys, who all served with distinction in World War One. From left to right are Norman (b.1893), who served in the R.A.S.C., Frank (b.1887) of the 1st (S) Battalion, Royal Guernsey Light Infantry, Thomas (b.1892) of the Royal Irish and R.G.L.I., and Eustace (b.1891) of the Royal Army Veterinary Corps and a well known veterinary surgeon in Guernsey. Thomas was killed in action at Cambrai in 1917 and Frank and Eustace both won the Military Cross. Seated from left to right are Dorothy, Edith, Alice and Irene. On the ground in front is May.

49. Eugene Thomas Lainé, manager of the Guernsey Old Bank. The Guernsey Banking Company merged with the National Provincial Bank in 1924. In 1970 it became the National Westminster Bank.

50. Guernsey's first qualified veterinary surgeon was Eustace J. Lainé, M.R.C.V.S. He is seen here standing outside his residence at 'Edgeborough', The Grange.

51. The bible class at the Vale Avenue Methodist church in 1911, a year after it was opened. The church later became a cinema and is now a garage.

52. Pupils who attended the Castel School in 1914. Back row: H. Le Tissier, M. Le Ray, E. J. De Garis, E. Duquemin, E. Gallienne, W. Le Tissier, P. Guille, –. Second row: V. Gardner, W. Le Page, B. Tough, J. Ferbrache, J. Hantonne, S. Le Cras, – Allett, N. Ferbrache, –. Third row: F. Le Parmentier, O. Guille, P. Carter, W. Carré, – Allett, E. Le Prevost, E. Lainé, E. Enevoldsen, E. Brouard, C. Enevoldsen. Front row: –, H. De Garis, F. Syvret, H. Le Parmentier, R. Le Noury, W. Moullin, W. Guilbert, C. Le Sauvage.

53. Charles Smith and his wife, Sophie, lived at Little St John Street, St Peter Port, where Mr. Smith ran his own business as a master carpenter. The Smiths had five sons, all of whom served in the army during the First World War. From left to right are Thomas (Royal Guernsey Light Infantry), William, Harold (R.G.L.I.), Arthur and Charles (R.G.L.I.). All returned unscathed from the conflict.

54. Gerald Basil Edwards (1899-1976), author of the unusual and outstanding novel *The Book of Ebenezer Le Page*, published in 1981. He is photographed with his Guernsey friend, Clarie Bellot (standing). Edwards was a Guernseyman who became a pupil-teacher. Between 1915-19 he served with the Royal Guernsey Light Infantry, and then went to Bristol University until 1923. He exiled himself from Guernsey in about 1926, wrote plays and visited the island on several occasions after the last war, when he lived for a while with Steve Picquet at his bunker home 'On Me Own', Pleinmont.

55.   In the 1920s Moullin's Tea Rooms were a well-known institution at Rue de la Lague, Rocquaine, St Peter-in-the-Wood. The large marquee was erected in a field near the house in order to cope with Sunday School picnics, and events such as the Rocquaine regatta .The Moullins also catered for the West Show, when it was held at Les Islets.

56.   Members of the Guernsey Farmers' Association at Les Touillets, Castel, during the 1920s. The group includes Tom Vidamour, W. Guilbert, J. N. Robin, Charles Kitts, P. Martel, Henry Carré, Ernest J. De Garis, W. H. Foote, O. Priaulx, Arthur W. Bell (Bailiff) and Osmond Le Page.

57.   Saward School, St Saviour's, is now La Salle Paroissiale in La Grande Rue. It was named after a former Lieutenant-Governor, Major-General Michael Henry Saward (1899-1903). Standing on the right is Miss Leale, the schoolmistress, who lived at Rue à L'Or, St Saviour's.

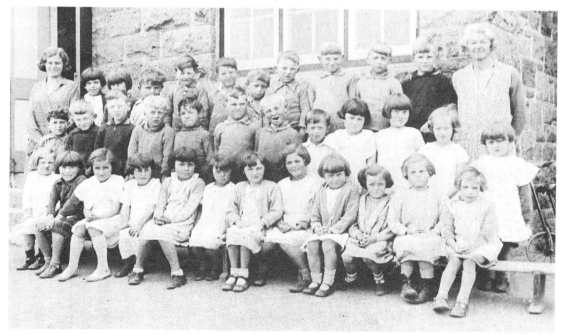

58.   When the States Water Board's new tower and tank at Haut Nez, Forest Road, was completed in November 1932, this photograph was taken of the board's 75 employees. Mr. A. A. Allain, the manager, reported 'not the slightest leak in the big tank of reinforced concrete', which stands 70 ft. above ground, is 415 ft. above sea level and holds 120,000 gallons. Water was pumped from Pré du Murie reservoir, St Pierre-du-Bois, to the tank, which enabled all houses to be 'supplied with a good head of water'.

59.   Officials and members of the Guernsey Agricultural and Horticultural Society, which for many years held an autumn show of fruit, vegetables and agricultural produce at St George's Hall. This photograph was probably taken in the early 1930s.

60. The days when poultry keepers could be numbered in their hundreds in Guernsey are gone. The Royal Guernsey Agricultural and Horticultural Society had a poultry section especially for them and organised an annual dinner. The fourth person on the right wearing the spectacles is William Vaudin, the *Evening Press* chief reporter. This photograph was taken in the 1930s.

61. The Sunnyside Tea Rooms at Vazon, a well-known place for refreshment before the Second World War. Standing on the right are Mr. and Mrs. George Howe.

62.   A meeting of the feudal court of Fief Le Compte took place in March 1937 at the court house, St George, Les Delisles, Castel. The photograph shows (left to right) John A. Bourgaise (sergeant), T. M. Vidamour (vavasseur de Longues), Captain L. Le M. Hutchesson (guest), Helier de Garis (vavasseur des Reveaux), N. Q. Le Pelley (vavasseur du Pignon), Henri Le Lièvre (sergeant), Jurat J. Allès Simon (sénéschal), Percy G. Martel (prévôt), Colonel T. Hutchesson (seigneur), Jurat Ernest de Garis (vavasseur de la Cour), Peter Girard (vavasseur de Carteret) and E. T. P. Ozanne (vavasseur du Groignet).

Back row: FC Locke, G Staples, H Langlois, HJ Wallbridge, GO Le Noury, GO Taylor, EG Bioelle, DC Wallace, RJ Hancock, WH Walker, FJ Hubert, AE Collivet, CJ Le Cras, G Horrell, A Piprell, WG Hubert, TL Le Sauvage. Third row: F Mellanby, WC Le Huray, W Le Cras, EW Vaudin, PJ Carré, HC Mudge Jnr, GW Knight, GW Burrows, VC Guillemet, E Petersen, J Carré, RS Knight, WH Gillingham, WS Udle, SC Smith, HW Pomeroy. Second row: S Crabbe, B de Guerin, EW Dawe, AG Le Moignan, HC Mudge, RH Ingram, HB Lancaster, PC Malzard, BE Mauger, R Duquemin, W Mudge, F Donnelly, HG Bienvenue, AJ Edmonds, R Gardiner, WG Luscombe. Front row: JH Hunkin, HE Marquand, CE Agnew, CB Blampied, WD Oliver, A Dorey, E De Garis, WL Henderson, RC Harris, JW Dear.

63.   The Guernsey fire brigade during the German Occupation. This picture was taken at the brigade's headquarters, Town Arsenal, in 1942. It also includes members of the States Waterworks Company, the island's Board of Administration, Air Raid Precautions personnel and St John Ambulance staff.

64. (*Left*) The artist Arthur Royce Bradbury (1892-1977) and his wife lived in Poole, Dorset, but spent many summers in Sark, where he had a studio. He painted principally in watercolour and exhibited widely; examples of his work are to be seen at the Imperial War Museum and at Castle Cornet, Guernsey. He was also a craftsman and made many boat models.

65. (*Below*) A Bradbury oil painting of the Seigneur and Dame de Serk with their daughter, Jehanne.

66. (*Bottom left*) A Bradbury watercolour of the Sark mill.

67. (*Bottom right*) Scale model of Victor Coysh's Guernsey fishing boat, *L'Hirondelle*. Made by Arthur Bradbury in 1954, it measures 10 in. by 3⅓ in. and its rigging is complete in every way.

AGRICULTURE

68. Seven women, five men and a boy, together with a horse-drawn plough, are in this picture of a potato field being dug and picked. One woman is wearing a Guernsey 'scoop' bonnet and most are wearing long rough aprons.

69. In 1876 the owner and breeder of this cow, Leader's Polly du Valet, was T. B. Le Prevost of Les Delisles, Castel, whose record at seven years old, when Norman Grut photographed her, was: milk, 14,230.25 lb; butter fat, 763.05 lb; and average butter fat, 5.36 lb.

70. In the days when Guernsey milk cost 4d. a pint, the milk lady delivered it by hand, pouring it from measure to jug.

71. Butter, in round one-pound pats, was often on sale in the public markets, where each pat bore the farmer's individual stamp and usually rested on dark green cabbage leaves.

72.- 75.   In 1803 the States purchased from André Batiste part of a field near Castel church for use as a fair field; previously the Michaelmas fair had been held on unenclosed land nearby. Following the formation of the Agricultural Society in 1817 the new fair field was used for cattle shows. It was last used for the King's Cups competition in 1948.

72.   Nicholas Le Beir (right) of 'Wisteria', King's Mills, was a major in the North Regiment, Royal Guernsey Militia and secretary of the Agricultural Society (1842-57). He died in 1859, and an obelisk was unveiled to his memory at Fairfield at the 1863 midsummer fair.

73.   The committee of the Royal Guernsey Agricultural and Horticultural Society and judges at the 1882 Whitsuntide cattle show. Colonel William Bell, C.B., was the society's president between 1874 and 1913.

74. Presentation of the King's Cups at Fairfield in 1910 by Mr. Osmond Priaulx (president of the Royal Guernsey Agricultural and Horticultural Society), fourth from left. Mr. Nico Ogier (second from left) is holding the cup for bulls. On the extreme right, holding a large cup, is Mr. Simon of La Câche, St Saviour's, who also won a cup for bulls. The man with a boater tilted on his head is the winner of the cup for cows.

75. The three prominent farmers standing with their animals in the front of this picture taken at a show at Fairfield in the 1920s are P. D. Ozanne of Les Pelleys, E. H. Ogier of Duveaux Farm and Osmond Le Page of Le Briquet. The island's first agricultural society was formed in 1817, with the first recorded export of cows in 1819. In 1842 this society was wound up and the Royal Guernsey Agricultural and Horticultural Society formed. Following a visit by H.M. Queen Victoria and Prince Albert in 1846 a cow and calf were sent to Osborne House, Isle of Wight. In 1871 exports started to the U.S.A., and in 1888 Queen Victoria presented the Queen's Cup for cows and bulls to the society, a competition still held every summer.

76. Henry and Elizabeth Drillot farmed 40 vergées of land at La Croix, where they kept eight cows and a few heifers. The farm was rebuilt in about 1920. This photograph shows Elizabeth Drillot milking one of the cows. She is wearing a traditional scoop bonnet.

77. Henry Drillot in the uniform of a Guernsey militiaman, photographed by T. A. Grut. Mr. Drillot was a blacksmith as well as a farmer, with a forge at La Croix where he shod both horses and oxen.

78. Caroline Drillot (Henry Drillot's grandmother) with Amanda, daughter of Henry and Elizabeth. Amanda, now Mrs. Moullin, lives at Doulieu, Le Mont Saint, St Saviour's.

79. This cow, Rose, was presented to King George V and Queen Mary by Ernest De Garis on behalf of the islanders at Saumarez Park in 1921. Holding the animal is Mr. De Garis' son, Ernest John De Garis, then aged seventeen.

80. All his life Jurat Ernest De Garis, O.B.E. (left) was a leading light in the island's dairy farming industry. A familiar figure at cattle shows in the Bailiwick, he was honorary secretary of the Royal Guernsey Agricultural and Horticultural Society from 1921. In 1954 he was elected president and was a recognised authority on the Guernsey breed. He exported cattle to many parts of the world and judged shows in the United Kingdom, the U.S.A. and Canada. A member of the States of Deliberation for 43 years, he died in 1955, aged 78. Here he is seen with Mr. N. Brehaut, another prominent local breeder.

81. As early as 1938 the Emergency Purposes Agricultural Committee had been set up to plan the export of produce in the event of war. On 1 July 1940 German forces occupied Guernsey, and soon afterwards the States Controlling Committee appointed Raymond O. Falla as agricultural officer. He set up and appointed the Farmers' Board to look after the interests of every farmer and grower in the island. Wilfred Bird and Theo Allez were given the job of looking after the collection and distribution of potatoes – a vital crop in those days. The board members were: –Robilliard, H. Ogier (St Sampson's), Emile Dorey (Castel), R. G. Froome (St Martin's), A. J. Le Patourel (St Peter Port), Peter Girard (Castel), John Bourgaize (St Saviour's), Fred Browning (St Andrew's), J. B. Tostevin (Torteval), Norman Collas (Vale), – Rawlinson, Wilson Gaudion (clerk), Ernest De Garis (chairman), R. O. Falla, Arthur Mahy, John Dorey, Wilfred Hubert and Frederick Heaume.

82. In 1942 Mr. Clifford Moullin, a well-known architect, was in charge of a potato depot at Doulieu, St Saviour's. The group shown here sorted potatoes brought in from growers who were permitted to retain a certain weight of their crop. The remainder had to be sold to the States for sale to islanders who relied heavily on the potato as food during the Occupation. Back row (left to right): Tom Brouard, Cliff Moullin, John Martel, Henry Girard, – Martel. Front row: Mabel Ozanne, Tom Tostevin, Amelia Drillot and Basil Ozanne.

83. Significant areas of the island were devoted to the growing of grain during and after the Occupation to help feed the human and animal population. Farmers took their wheat to the Charroterie Mills (now demolished) and to J. Bragg and Sons for milling. Rex Bragg ground about 300 tons of oats in 1941. Grain was also imported from Alderney and Sark. This photograph was taken at George Dorey's farm, Le Lorier, St Saviour's, in 1958. Threshing went on for several days, during which time neighbouring farmers also brought their grain.

HORTICULTURE

84. At a time when the tomato was grown in almost every glasshouse, this was not an unusual sight. This man is delivering tomato baskets to a vinery. Each basket held 12 lb of tomatoes, and hundreds of thousands were made for the scores of agents who set up business for the export of fruit to the United Kingdom.

85. Greenhouse workers at L'Eclet Vinery, St Saviour's, *c.*1916. On the left of the truck loaded with freshly picked tomatoes are Dick Corbin, Nick Pinchmain and George Nicholson. The boy in front is Walter Le Moigne, who was then aged about seven. He earned 10 shillings (50p) a week, nine of which he gave to his mother. On the right are Fred –, Gerald James from the Longfrie, –, and Jim Le Ray.

86. The Le Couteur brothers, George and Edmund, who were tomato growers of Le Coudré, St Pierre-du-Bois, also imported thousands of wicker baskets for the trade from France. These were marked with the initials of U.K. salesmen and delivered to growers. Those shown here each held 12 lb and had a lid which had to be tied on. In addition, a distinctive tag was attached to every basket with the name and address of the salesman. Hundreds of thousands of these tags were produced by local printers. Other baskets in different shapes were made for grapes. The Le Couteurs had a large store in Hospital Lane, St Peter Port, and another at Le Coudré, known as Le Grand Bâtiment, where this photograph was taken.

87. The Fruit Export Company was first established at the White Rock, St Peter Port, in 1904 and retained premises there until after the Second World War. In the 1920s the firm acquired additional premises at Les Banques and became a limited company. The sheds were then solely used for the manufacture and storage of fruit baskets and flower boxes. One shed, which is now the horticultural shop, was originally an aircraft hangar near Cirencester. It had been shipped to Guernsey and was re-erected in 1921.

88a. & b. Duveaux Farm, St Sampson's, was once famous for its figs, which were grown extensively along with crops of beans, shown here under glass. Figs were still being exported to T. J. Poupart Ltd., Covent Garden, during the 1960s.

89. Workers in a glasshouse of carnations at Les Jetteries, St Saviour's, where every operation was done by hand. The boys in the foreground are each holding a watering can.

90. In 1863 Charles Smith of Caledonia Nursery, Fosse André, St Peter Port, started the export trade in flowers when he sent camellias to Covent Garden. From that time onward, Guernsey flowers of all kinds have been seen on the wholesale and retail markets of the U.K. Chrysanthemums such as these were shipped by the thousand.

TRADE AND INDUSTRY

91.   The first newspaper to be printed in Guernsey was *Gazette de L'Ile de Guernsey* on Saturday 8 January 1791. In 1842 it became *La Gazette Officielle*. In 1934 this was published as a supplement to the *Star*, which itself had been published since 1813. In 1824 Nicholas Mauger became the sole proprietor, followed by his daughter Charlotte in 1855. Her son, Thomas Mauger Bichard (on the far left in the photograph), took over in 1860. He was a captain in the North Regiment, Royal Guernsey Militia. The woman standing next to him was probably his first wife (*née* Martha de la Rue) who died in 1887. Next to her is their son, Herbert Mauger Bichard, who died in 1907. The seven men in aprons were the compositors, who hand-set the type for the newspaper. This photograph was taken outside the *Gazette and Advertiser* premises at 2 Bordage Street, St Peter Port.

92. 'Araucaria', Les Varendes, was Thomas Mauger Bichard's St Andrew's home.

93. Wardley's printing works, 1910. Originally based in Mansell Street, they later moved to Rectory House, now the offices of the Channel Islands Co-operative Society Ltd., where for many years they printed the States Telephone Directory. The printer on the left is standing at a 'stone', holding a mallet. The other three are operating flat bed and platen hand-fed printing machines.

94. Box carts and horses were common in the heyday of the quarries in the Vale and St Sampson's. Granite was shattered into manageable blocks and hauled from the quarry floor to the summit by a 'blondin' crane. It was then taken by box cart to the crushing mill near St Sampson's harbour. One of the principal firms engaged in this work was A. & F. Manuelle, whose horse and cart is seen in this rare photograph. The firm's stables, which still exist, were in Grandes Maisons Road and their horses grazed in the fields of Bulwer Avenue. Manuelle's ceased operations in Guernsey in 1969 after the major landslide at their Longue Hougue quarry.

95. Le Riche's, wine and spirit merchants in High Street and Lefebvre Street, used to bottle their own alcohol in their extensive cellars, into which over one hundred barrels were laboriously lowered by rope from street level each year. The building was once part of Le Manoir de Haut (now the Constables' Office), built in 1787 by the Le Marchant family.

96. The once-familiar steam-driven roller has long since disappeared from island roads, together with the gangs of road menders with their picks, shovels and forks.

97. Frederick Coysh was a coach-builder, whose 'Paragon Coach Works' was at Park Street. He also repaired and painted cycles. An 1885 advertisement stated, 'carriages of every description built to order. Painting and trimming executed with neatness and despatch'. The workshop closed in about 1920, when motor cars started to oust horse-drawn vehicles. One of his 'caravans' – a closed wagonette – is now at the island's Folk Museum. Mr. Coysh was also the bandmaster of the Artillery Band (Militia). He died in 1925, at the age of eighty.

98. Victoria House, 17 and 19 High Street, in 1905. This was the thriving drapery and costume business of Abraham Bishop. In 1921 it was sold to Creasey and Son, but continued under the original name. Bishop's announced a closing down sale on 11 November 1932, when flannel shirts could be bought for 2s. 4d. and carpenters' aprons for 11½d. The photograph shows the Bishop's staff standing outside Bishop's premises.

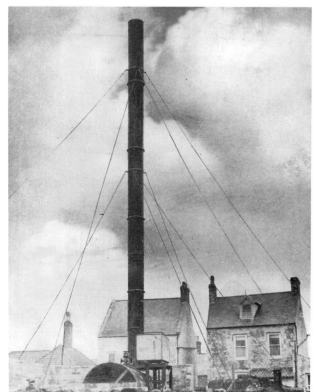

99. In 1935 this was probably the highest chimney in Guernsey. It was erected by Burgess and Son of Nocq Road, St Sampson's. The 65-ft. chimney was for a laundry being established by Peter Kinnersly. The site is now part of the Channel Islands Co-operative Ltd. supermarket.

100.-102. At the beginning of this century a campaign for a sub-post office at St Saviour's led to the 1906 opening of one in the Grande Rue run by Mr. J. Miller, baker and grocer, who also had interests in public transport. These premises became a receiving house for letters and parcels only, which were collected by the postman. Although a rubber date stamp was sent to Guernsey on 22 February 1906, this was used mainly as a receiving stamp.

By 1911 the sub-post office was situated at Cleveland, Rue des Crabbes, where today Mr. Sam Allett runs a dairy farm. It was run, together with a drapery and grocery business, by Mr. W. W. Blondel. His assistant was Miss Gertrude Jehan, the mother of the present owner. Miss Jehan's father was a butcher, so fresh pork was also sold. Outside the old shop is a ring in the wall to which horses were tied.

The present sub-post office and stores was built in 1915, when Mr. and Mrs. Sullivan took over. In 1923 it was acquired by Mr. and Mrs. Thomas Ogier Bichard, and in 1957 by Mr. and Mrs. Reginald Ashplant.

THE TROUBLES OF A COUNTRY POSTMAN

'I REALLY CAN'T TAKE ANY MORE'

100. (*Above*) This cartoon by J. S. Irish appeared in the *Guernsey Evening Press* and sparked the move towards the parish having its own sub-post office. It was accompanied by a letter suggesting that St Saviour's people should give the postmen so much to do that they would quarrel with their employers 'and thus compel alterations in the present unsatisfactory state of affairs'.

101. (*Left*) Perelle supply stores and post office, when it was run by Mrs. Sullivan (second from left) and her husband (standing beside their car). The lamp was lit by oil. The thatch on the distant cottage was burned down in about 1934.

102. The post office was also a general store, as can be seen from the array of goods in the window.

103.   Arthur J. Torode was apprenticed as a quarry blacksmith at the Ville Baudu, Vale. He earned two shillings a week
at the age of fifteen. During the First World War he worked at Beaucette Quarry (now the Channel Islands Yacht Marina).
He joined the Quarry Company and went to France with the Royal Engineers. Mr. Torode is seen here working at a forge
at La Hure Mare, Vale. He died in 1982.

TRANSPORT

104. A rare photograph of a Royal Mail cart rounding the corner at the top of St Julian's Avenue. The cart, with uniformed driver and assistant, is decorated with a floral crown and bears the date 1897. This indicates that it was probably about to participate in celebrations connected with the diamond jubilee of Queen Victoria.

105. This charming picture shows Etta Paint of La Houguette, St Pierre-du-Bois, who married Thomas Mansell Simon of Les Câches, St Saviour's. The baby seated on the donkey is Gladys Simon.

106.   A Renault car of *c.*1909 at the top of the Grange, where the chauffeur has probably just stopped to pick up passengers. The coachwork may well have been locally built and intended to be part of a horse-drawn vehicle.

107.   For those who could afford it, a trip to Jersey by sea provided a welcome break. Three people from Guernsey – Louie Le Couteur, Tom Simon (second from left in the front) and Edmund Le Couteur with the bowler hat – were in Jersey on a coach tour when Albert Smith took this picture.

108. Trinity Bakery, Mansell Street, which is now part of Jim Langlois Ltd. William Cluett established a bakery in 1777. Stabling for the horses was in Contrée Mansell where L'Atelier now is. The horse, Brownie, was sold to Mr. Sarre of St Brioc, St Pierre-du-Bois, on 16 December 1909. The photograph was taken alongside Trinity Church.

109. This photograph was taken at the Weighbridge, St Peter Port, where the offices of the London and South Western Railway once stood. It shows the staff of the company about to set off on a picnic in wagonettes on 12 September 1917. The buildings behind were demolished in 1974 and replaced by Manufacturers Hanover House and Lazard House.

110. Numerous accidents occurred on this corner of the Charroterie, where the road became a bottleneck and a high wall obscured the view. In 1935 an illuminated warning sign was erected. The Germans also found this corner difficult to negotiate with large gun transporters, and solved the problem by demolishing the wall and rebuilding it further back.

111. In 1935 almost every glasshouse in Guernsey was steam sterilised. Boilers such as this could be seen throughout the winter months, travelling from vinery to vinery where steam under pressure was injected into the soil to kill pests and diseases.

112. These four lorries had just arrived at the White Rock for the Southern Railway and Great Western Railway Companies in 1938.

SPORT

113. An enormous crowd gathered at L'Ancresse Common on 23 July 1908 for the annual race meeting. There were six races. One owner brought his horse from Jersey and there were numerous visitors from that island. The Guernsey Cup (one mile, four runners), went to the owner of 'Blazes', Mr. A. T. Jeremie, who had won it on three previous occasions. There were side shows and a living Aunt Sally – a man in a barrel wearing a top hat. The evening entertainments were also popular: a thousand people attended 'The Gaieties' concert party at Candie, and there was another large gathering at Les Terres Gardens and a variety show at St Julian's Hall.

114. Although omnibuses were operating to L'Ancresse to convey people to the races there were many who went in hired wagonettes. There were also some automobiles. Picnics on the grass were the order of the day and James Travers of the Prince of Wales Royal Restaurant, 'the well known champion caterer of the world', was serving lobster lunches at 2s. 6d. in a specially fitted marquee. F. W. Guérin was there to record the event with his camera.

115. Arthur James Maunder (1854-1932) was an enthusiastic cricketer, a good left-handed bowler and a member of the Grange Club. In this photograph he is second from the left on the centre row with, to his left, Dr. Conrad Carey. Fourth from the left on the back row is C. J. H. Rawlinson, and to his right is Frank Mourant.

116 Arthur Maunder was also a great cycling enthusiast who, at the age of 25, set up a cycle business at 18 and 20 Pollet. He was deeply involved with the Guernsey Bicycle and Tricycle Club, with whom he won many prizes. In 1884 he became club champion. He also raced in Jersey, where a certain bend in the course was known as 'Maunder's Corner'.

GUERNSEY
Bicycle & Tricycle Club.

SECOND ANNUAL SPORTS

Will take place on the

NEW TRACK on the CASTLE EMPLACEMENT

On

THURSDAY, AUGUST 27, 1885,

Under the distinguished Patronage and Presence of
His Excellency

MAJ.-GEN. H. A. SAREL, C.B.,

LIEUTENANT-GOVERNOR, and

MRS. SAREL,

EDGAR MACCULLOCH, ESQ., F.R.A.S.,

BAILIFF,

J. T. R. De HAVILLAND, Esq.,

JURAT,

JULIUS A. CAREY & J. B. MARQUAND, Esqs.,

HIGH CONSTABLES,

Col. KARSLAKE and OFFICERS of H.M.'s.

ROYAL IRISH RIFLES,

Col. JONES & OFFICERS

Of the R.G.A. ARTILLERY.

By the kind permission of Col. JONES the BAND of the Regiment will attend and play a choice selection of Music during the afternoon under the direction of Bandmaster COYSH.

PROGRAMME.

March .... "The Castle of Stirling" .... *T. Kelly*
Quadrille .... " Ida" .... *G. Cheesman*
Waltz .... "Fairy Land" .... *W. T. Harris*
March .... " In the Ranks" .... *H. Fogarty*
Lancers ...... "Knight of the Garter" ...... *Vandervell*
Galop .... " Always Jolly" .... *Lyons*
Quadrille .... "Good as Gold" .... *Jones*
Polka .... "The First Rose" .... *Unsworth*
Waltz .... " Emerald" .... *H. Round*
March .... " Blue Eyed Fisherboy" .... *Shaw*
GOD SAVE THE QUEEN.

At One o'clock the Track will be formally opened by His Excellency Maj.-Gen. H. A. SAREL. At Six o'clock the Prizes will be delivered by His Excellency and Mrs. SAREL.

SPORTS to commence at 1.30 p.m.

COMMITTEE:

JULIUS A. CAREY, Esq., President; Mr. A. ROGER, Vice-President; Messrs. A. MAUNDER, H. G. LE CHEMINANT, W. S. GRANT and W. MARTIN.

Judge.—Mr. J. BISHOP.

Starter.—Mr. R. HONEY.

Time-Keeper.—Mr. A. LE CHEMINANT.

Referees.—Messrs. COOPER, H. J. LE CHEMINANT and N. BROUARD.

Lap-Keepers.—Messrs. C. M. BROUARD & R. ROWCLIFFE.

Hon. Secs.—Messrs. J. A. CRESSARD & F. McD. JAGO.

PRICE TWOPENCE.

The Public are requested to keep their dogs at home.

117.   Guernsey Bicycle and Tricycle Club programme.

118.   The above programme requested the public to keep their dogs at home. What might have happened had the request been ignored is depicted in this pen and ink sketch by Graham Marriette.

GIVE A DOG A BONE SHAKER ....

119.   The St Pierre-du-Bois Air Rifle Club, winners of the B.S.A. Cup, 1925-26. Back row (left to right): W. J. Queripel, J. A. De Garis, T. Corbin, A. B. Corbin, S. D. Brehaut, J Bourgaize. Front row: T. W. Tostevin, A. T. Roberts, T. R. Lenfestey (captain), J. Gallienne, G. Le M. Le Couteur.

120.   This is the final of the first competition for the Pyramids Cup (La Rapide Trophy) which took place at the Sarnian Club on 5 December 1935. The finalists were T. Baker and A. E. Zabiela, both former island billiards champions. In the photograph are, from left to right: H. H. McBean, A. E. Zabiela, W. Edwards, E. Stead, J. Ross, T. Baker and J. Le Maitre.

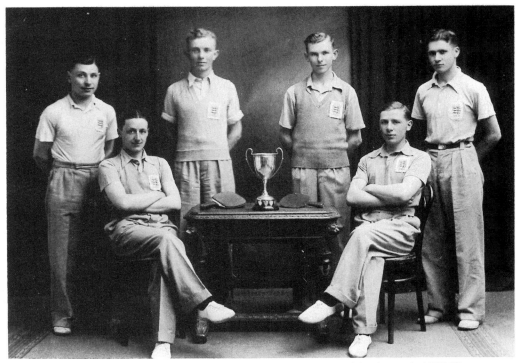

121. The Guernsey Island table tennis team were winners of the Green Trophy for this inter-island event in 1937. The team consisted of Robert Herpe, Bert Brenton (captain), Clifford Guilbert, Richard Denziloe, Wilfred Denning (reserve) and Lloyd Strappini. Strictly called the Royal Yacht Hotel Trophy, it was presented by Albert Green in March 1926, and was originally intended to be competed for by the leading clubs of Guernsey and Jersey. Playing at home during the first season in 1926, Guernsey beat Jersey's First Tower team at the Guille-Allès Artisans' Institute, Market Street. Bert Brenton was Guernsey's star player, and became island champion on no fewer than 20 occasions. Before the German Occupation the trophy was buried in Mr. Strappini's garden for the duration of hostilities.

122. The Old Intermedians water polo team, winners of the Williams' Trophy in 1937. Back row: F. J. Hubert, S. Gaved, G. Naftel, H. Olliver, H. Nicolle. Front row: J. Davidson, G. V. Guilbert (captain), R. Naftel (vice-captain), R. Nicolle.

123. Young members of the Guernsey Riding Club about to set out from Manor Farm, St Martin's, shortly before the Second World War. From left to right are: Mary and Peter Dorey, Nancy Noel, Graham Froome, and David and Dianne Bougourd.

124. The Elizabeth College team which met Victoria College in July 1939 at the College Field. From left to right, standing, are: – Borne, R. L. S. Bichard, L. C. Siedle, G. J. B. Green, – McMaster, – Dorey. Sitting: R. Batiste, B. W. Rose, W. C. Watling (captain), R. P. Collas, E. J. Hillier.

125. Joe Davis, the world snooker champion, in an opening session in 1939 against Horace Lindrum, the Australian champion. The event took place at the *Channel Islands* (now the *Savoy*) *Hotel*.

126. (*Right*) The first open fishing competition organised by the Guernsey Sea Anglers' Club, the year before the club was formally constituted in 1938. Over 100 people entered this first event, on the west side of the New Jetty, St Peter Port. Rules were simple: rod or line, and only one hook for each angler.

127. (*Below*) In July 1939 the Guernsey Kolapore team and other marksmen were at Bisley. From left to right are: Lieutenant-Colonel R. W. Randall (team captain), H. K. Falla, Dr. E. F. Aubert, J. Smith, F. J. Cope, A. Littlefield, H. N. Falla, D. Bisset, E. Despointes, A. Domaille, A. Young, W. P. Mahy, H. Bean. Hanging from the top of the scoreboard are three bunches of Guernsey tomatoes. England beat Canada to win the cup by six points, with an aggregate score of 1,107.

EVENTS

128.   Parochial processions to celebrate the capture of Guy Fawkes in 1605 were noisy affairs throughout the island. This group, together with a volunteer fife and drum band, is about to set off from the Huyshe Memorial building, near the *Last Post*, St Andrew's. False beards and blackened faces were the order of the day. The band was led by a horseman, and an effigy of Guy Fawkes was carried in procession around the parish to end at a burning ground. Locally the event is still known as Budloe night, the word 'budloe' being derived from *bout de l'an*, when a log was once ceremoniously burned on New Year's Eve. This photograph was taken by M. J. Cluett during the late 19th century.

129. This enormous arch in honour of the coronation of King George V in 1911 spanned the junction of St Sampson's Bridge and New Road. The premises in the centre belonged to the grocer, E. Brehaut. Although some of the buildings have survived, post-war development to the left has considerably altered the scene.

130. In 1911 Mr. E. J. Honey decorated his engineering premises on St Sampson's Bridge with electric lights in honour of the coronation. Mr. Honey – who was also a coppersmith – was standing with his staff at the shop entrance. On the right was part of F. H. C. Wright's butcher's shop, which now sells electrical goods.

131.   In August 1915 the 9th Bertozerie Scout Troop held a picnic at Pleinmont. The bell tent behind indicates that they may have been camping.

132.   The diamond jubilee of the Sion Sunday School, Les Brehauts, St Pierre-du-Bois, took place in July 1922. It was photographed by Thomas Bramley.

133. Mystery drives were the vogue before the Second World War. This shows buses and open-topped charabancs about to set off from outside the States Office. The destination was kept secret. Often those taking part were encouraged to follow a set of clues in order to find their prizes.

134. With his bowler hat resting on a pile of boxes near a marquee the Bailiff of Guernsey, Sir Victor G. Carey, cuts the first sod of turf near the Forest Road at La Villiaze on 20 September 1937. This signalled the start of work on the island's airport which was officially opened on 6 May 1939 by Sir Kingsley Wood. Ninety-two acres of land had to be levelled, including around 70 fields and five miles of hedges.

135. There were many poor children in Guernsey before the Second World War. Those shown here in 1935 were being given free dinners at the Notre Dame du Rosaire schools. This was made possible through the generosity of La Société Francaise de Bienfaisance.

136. During the excavations for the reservoir dam at St Saviour's in 1939, heavy rain caused serious flooding. The fire brigade took 'Sarnia' to the scene to pump out the unwanted lake.

137.   During the First World War the Royal Guernsey Militia was encamped at what is now the car park at Grandes Rocques, adjacent to the *Grandes Rocques Hotel*, which had been run by Mr. and Mrs. Claude Way for 50 years. During the war a violent storm blew up and flattened most of the tents, causing chaos. Where Le Riche's supermarket now stands were the Terminus Tea Rooms, run by Dan Le Cheminant. On the nearby sand dunes rested an ancient upturned boat in which lived a bearded old man.

138. In 1953 the monument to the memory of Sir John Doyle, Lieutenant-Governor of Guernsey 1803-16, was rebuilt at Jerbourg following its destruction by German forces. The firm of George Le M. Le Couteur was contracted to do the work. Following its completion, a new direction indicator was mounted on a granite stone which had been erected by the ratepayers of St Martin's to commemorate the coronation of King George VI on 12 May 1937. Performing the ceremony was the Bailiff, Sir Victor Carey. Among those present were W. G. Luscombe (constable), Guy Blampied, General C. de Sausmarez, B. G. Blampied and Frank Le Page (both douzeniers).

139. Rebuilding the monument to Sir John Doyle in 1953.

140.   On the 18th anniversary of Liberation Day, 9 May 1963, the Women's Royal Voluntary Service formed a guard of honour at Government House when Her Majesty the Queen Mother visited Guernsey. His Excellency the Lieutenant-Governor, Admiral Sir Geoffrey Robson, who died in 1990, was in attendance.

141.   An inspection of the crew of the lifeboat *Queen Victoria* by Princess Alexandra, the Duchess of Kent and The Hon. Angus Ogilvy in 1968. On the left is the Bailiff, Sir William Arnold, who accompanied the royal couple. In the background are Captain J. C. Allez, the harbourmaster, and Mr. B. G. Blampied, O.B.E., chairman of the lifeboat committee. The crew on this occasion comprised John Petit (cox), Wilf Savident, Jack Le Page, Eric Pattimore (engineer), Bob Vowles and Ronnie Munson.

The Second World War

142. Shortly before the declaration of war against Germany on 3 September 1939, this was the scene at Fermain Bay.
About 50 boats were counted when this photograph was taken.

143. A few days before the outbreak of war in Europe in September 1939, over 40,000 gas masks had been assembled for
the population by 50 students of Elizabeth College and 40 island scouts. The headquarters for this operation was St Paul's
Church, St James' Street. Church halls and schools throughout the island were used as depots from which islanders
collected their masks, each carefully packed in cardboard boxes.

144a. & b.   In the autumn of 1939, after war had been declared against Germany, the Guernsey Air Raid Precautions Committee asked all motorists to paint their car bumpers white and instructed that all side lamp reflectors be blacked. Two thicknesses of tissue paper also had to be placed in front of the bulb. Headlamps had to be covered with a metal cover with a slit and hood, to ensure that no light was visible more than eight paces away. The tops of all lamps containing a red glass had to be blackened. Motor House Ltd. had organised this demonstration model, which stood in Smith Street.

145. Ration books being prepared for distribution in St Paul's, a former Methodist church.

146. Life went on apparently as usual at La Vallette bathing pools during the long hot summer of 1940, the year the Germans invaded Guernsey. The diving stage was deemed to be dangerous during the 1980s and has been removed.

147. A Martin Bros. delivery van in High Street in 1940. It travelled the island delivering tobacco and cigarettes until supplies were curtailed. Mr. Frank Martin is standing on the left.

148. The bombing of St Peter Port by the Germans in June 1940 caused most windows in the States Office to be blown out. As a result it was decided to evacuate the staff of civil servants and install them temporarily at Saumarez Park, now the Hostel of St John. Some of them appear in this photograph. Back row: F. W. McCrea, H. W. Smith, George Blondel, John Dowding, George Clarke, George Le Quesne, Vaughan Cooper, Cyril Duquemin. Centre row: Marjorie Keyho, Marion Duquemin, Ivy Balcombe, Thelma Smith, –, Mrs. Duquemin, Vernon Le Maître, C. Hamon. Front row: George Higgs, –, W. Frampton, Christine Neville, H. E. Marquand (States Supervisor), Mary Bird, E. F. Lainé, Nancy Marquand and Harold Brache.

149. Refugees from the north of France who arrived in Guernsey by fishing boat early in June 1940, shortly before the Germans. This photograph was taken outside the *Savoy Hotel*.

150. Meat was severely rationed during the Occupation. Here housewives wait patiently for Jory's charcuterie to open in the Pollet.

151. These fishermen were washing seaweed (carrageen moss) which was dried, ground into flour and used for making blancmange or mixing with other food. The chemist J. N. Carré produced a booklet of customers' recipes for using flavoured coloured carrageen powder. The collection of seaweed was stopped when the German forces mined the beaches to deter Allied landings.

152. (*Above*) The Guernsey Brewery, South Esplanade, soon ran out of beer. When this photograph was taken in 1941 all these barrels had been emptied by the Germans.

153. (*Above*) A carved wooden sign outside a German army hairdresser's.

154. (*Left*) A mock hanging of Adolf Hitler took place at the *Channel Islands Hotel* soon after the island was liberated.

ALDERNEY

155. In 1847 the British Government began work on a 'harbour of refuge' in Braye Bay, Alderney, as a counter measure against the French who had built enormous defence works just 25 miles away at Cherbourg. Alderney was to be a naval station, a counterpart to Portland. The work of building a breakwater and forts went on for 30 years. This photograph shows British destroyers sheltering in Braye Bay in June 1906.

156. The building of Alderney Lighthouse (otherwise known as 'Mannez', but pronounced 'Moanay') was completed in 1912. In September 1910 Trinity House invited tenders for its construction and William Baron of Alderney received the contract.

157. The S.S. *Buoyant* alongside the Douglas Quay, Alderney, in 1930. The crew apparently abandoned ship in 'The Swinge', a notoriously dangerous passage between Alderney and Burhou. The vessel was taken over by Alderney seafarer, Bonnie Newton, and another seafarer, who brought her safely into harbour.

158. The motor vessel *Guernseyman* was a familiar sight when she plied mixed cargoes between Guernsey, Alderney and Sark. She was built in Holland in 1938 and owned by Sark Motor Ships. In 1939 she was sold to a couple of adventurers who intended to sail round the world.

159. Jurats of the Court of Alderney in 1935. From left to right are: A. C. Tourgis, C. H. Richards, W. H. Mignot, J. M. Rapson and D. S. Le Cocq.

160.   Frederick George French (1889-1962) was appointed Judge of Alderney in the summer of 1938, following the death of Major R. W. Mellish. French resigned in 1947. He is seen here with his wife.

161. The first sitting of the Court of Alderney under Judge French, following his appointment in 1938.

162. Judge French inspecting the guard of honour of the Alderney branch of the British Legion in July 1938.

163. The presentation of prizes at the 1935 Alderney cattle show, to which Guernsey judges travelled each year.

164. A party of Guernsey people returning home from Alderney on the *Courier* in 1935. They had been to the northern island to see the annual cattle show.

165. The 1939 New Year's Eve cabaret at the *Marais Hall Hotel* in Alderney was presented by pupils of Miss C. Jefferies. It was the last such event for a very long time. The following June the island was evacuated and quickly occupied by German forces.

SARK

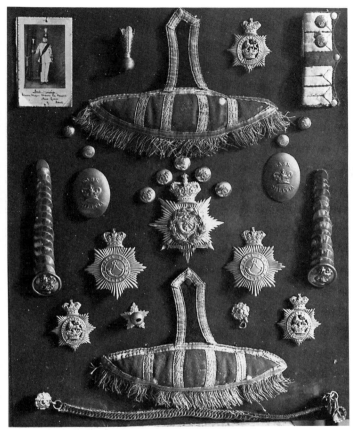

166. (*Above*) Insignia of the Royal Sark Militia collected by
R. P. Spencer and now in a museum in Castle Cornet. The militia
was disbanded in 1880.

167. (*Above right*) A Royal Sark Militia badge.

168. Drum Major Henri Le Feuvre of the Royal Sark Militia, *c.*1855.

169. Guernsey people on a day trip to Sark, Easter 1910.

170. In 1913 Havre Gosselin wall parapet and landing were rebuilt at a cost of £695. There were 41 steps leading to the small harbour on the west coast, which had originally been built in 1817. The work in 1913 was done by G. Le M. Le Couteur, the Guernsey contractors. Among those in the photograph are Walter, Eugene, Tom and Bertie Fallaize, S. Kellington, Abraham Le Noury, Jean Le Sauvage, William Le Lacheur and W. Baker.

171. If you take a lobster, stand it on its head and stroke its tail, it will remain stationary. Guy Blampied was about 10 years old when he visited Sark and was shown this trick by a young Sark boy. A feature about this 'act' appeared in *The Strand Magazine* about 80 years ago.

172. *Stock's Hotel*, Sark, had its own stables with horses which carried visitors and goods from the harbour. This early photograph shows Philip Le Feuvre and Guy Blampied of Guernsey as boys.

173. The annual Sark cattle show is still an event to which Guernsey judges are invited. Earlier in the century there were many more dairy farms in Sark than at present and the show was of greater significance. Here is a group of Guernsey and Sark officials at one of the early shows.

174. In 1931 Sark Chief Pleas decided that the main tunnel from Creux Harbour to the Harbour Hill was potentially dangerous because of falling stones. Messrs. Le Couteur of Guernsey gave an estimate of £1,248 for lining out the entire tunnel, and their tender was accepted. The work included projecting parapets as they are seen today. Workmen included in this picture are Charles Vibert, Walter Le Feuvre and Bill de Carteret, all of Sark.

175. La Coupée, the narrow road which links Big Sark with Little Sark, was in a sad state of repair after the Second World War. When the Occupation ended in 1945 the Royal Engineers used German prisoners-of-war to help them reconstruct the road in concrete. There is a 300-ft. sheer drop to the sea on either side of what was originally a gravel track with no railings. In high winds islanders had to crawl across on hands and knees.

176. Guernsey's Lieutenant-Governor Sir Charles Coleman with the Bishop of Winchester when they visited Sark in 1965.

177. The Pilcher Monument was erected on the west coast of Sark following the loss of an 18-ft. gig with five men on board which left Havre Gosselin for Guernsey in rough seas on the evening of 19 October 1868. The granite obelisk was built to their memory by the widow of Jeremiah Giles Pilcher, one of those drowned. In 1968 the monument was restored by the Guernsey builders, Phillips and Le Page.

Herm

178.   Lord Perry was the last Crown Tenant of Herm before the arrival of German forces in 1940. He was chairman of the Ford Motor Corporation. This photograph came from the collection of Hans Max Von Aufsess, who was head of civil affairs in the German Field Command.

179.   The States of Guernsey purchased the island of Herm for £15,000 in 1946 from H.M. Treasury. This photograph shows the States Board of Administration with their first tenant, Mr. A. J. Jefferies, standing on the extreme left. He came from Upton Lovel, Warminster, in Wiltshire. The lease was for 60 years, the first year's rent being £100, which had risen to £1,000 by the fifth year. By 1949 Mr. Jefferies found it impossible to continue and that year the tenancy was taken over by Major and Mrs. A. G. Wood, who have been there ever since. The photograph shows: Mr. Jefferies, Jurat Pierre de Putron, Jurat W. J. Sarre, Jurat Ernest De Garis, Mr. Ernest Lainé (States Engineer), Mr. H. E. Marquand (States Supervisor), Mr. Ron Short (secretary, States Finance Committee), Mr. Louis Guillemette (assistant supervisor) and the committee president, Jurat R. H. Johns. When the island was held by the Crown, Prince Blücher von Wahlstatt, Compton Mackenzie and Lord Perry were among the tenants.

PHOTOGRAPHERS

Photographs working in Guernsey between 1843 and c.1910

(The dates given are the earliest found in local almanacs and newspapers)

Alier, Mrs., Pollet, 1866
American Photo Company, 12 Smith Street, 1906
Amet, E., Captain, Havelet, 1861 André, 2 Victoria Road (Crescent), 1878
Angell, S., Vale Road, 1911

Bailey, 5 Pollet, 1861 (the studio was later run by his wife)
Banks, T. B. & Co.
Barber, A., Berthelot Street, 1843 Barbet, High Street, *c.*1870
Baudoux, E. & Sons, 1 North Clifton, 1885 (branch of Jersey firm)
Bienvenu, Cordier Hill, 1866-*c.*1870
Billinghurst and Downham, *c.*1890 (branch of Jersey firm)
Blondel, A., St Saviour's, 20th century
Bramley, Victoria Road, later 'Hiawatha', St Julian's Avenue, 20th century
Brown, Charles, Glategny, 1863
Burnside, James, 5 Pollet, 1886

Caire, N. J. (emigrated to Australia *c.*1860, opening a studio in Adelaide in 1867)
Cluett, M. J., Victoria Road, late 19th century
Cobdon, C. H. & Co., 4 Smith Street, late 19th century
Collenette, B., 15 Smith Street, 1878; 7 Union Street, 1894
Coombes, W. J., Mount Durand
Cumber, Miss, 3 Pollet, mid-1860s until mid-1880s
Dawson, W., 15 Les Amballes; opposite St John's School, *c.*1860
Dumaresq & Co., 3 St James' Street, 1890s
Dunn, H., Le Tourgand, North Esplanade, 1858 (his wife took over *c.*1886)

Ellis, Edward, St Jacques, 1867
Eureka & Co., late 19th century (manager: S. Stein)

Frances Brothers, 31 Victoria Road, *c.*1866-72 (formerly of 61 Great Russell Street, London)

Garnier, Arsène, 1848-1880s
Gee, C., Church Street, *c.*1859
Globe Photo Company, Vale Road
Grut, T. A., 2 Victoria Crescent, 1879-94; 5 Pollet, 1894
Grut, Norman, 5 Pollet
Guérin, F. W., freelance photographer, early 20th century
Guillon, 3 Vauvert, 1873

Hamson, J. A., St James' Street, 20th century
Henry, Gayter, 50 Victoria Road, 1876; later also used studio at 5 Pollet
Herival, J., 21 Mount Durand, *c*.1906
Hicks, 16 Vauvert, also 3 Vauvert, 1882
Hutchinson, 17 George Street, 1864
Hutton, T. B., 10 Grange and Candie, *c*.1863-1880s
Hyams, S., Charroterie

Jamouneau, A. J., Grange, 1891
Javelot, A., Wesley Road, 1861; later Victoria Road (Mrs. Javelot took over in 1870)
Javelot and Sarchet, St Sampson's, 1878

Kaines, H. J., St James' Street, late 19th century, early 20th century

Laurens, A., 19 Pollet, late 19th century, early 20th century
Lefeuvre, M., 24 Hauteville, 1847

Maguire, G., Saumarez Street, 1876
Maguire, J. (Maguire Brothers); later known as The Electric Light Studio, Grange
Mansell, Dr., 1860s
Marquand, W. I., Mansell Street, 1863; later Vauvert, until the 1880s
Mayhew, W. J., Forest Lane, 1872
Myers, William, Old Rectory, Market Place, 1861 until the late 1880s

Owen, 7 College Street

Le Page (late of Javelot and Sarchet), late 19th century and early 20th century
Peers, 18 Berthelot Street, 1842
Petit, J. P.

Rattenbury, I. D., 12 Mount Row, 1876
De La Rue, Warren, 1815-1889 (took early photographs of the moon; son of Thomas [1793-1866], founder of famous printing firm of banknotes and playing cards)

Singleton, Thomas, 1868; La Couture, 1870; Vauvert, 1872; Pollet, 1878; later, 3 Bellevue Terrace, Rohais
Singleton, H. J., 20th century
Stonelake, J. B., Les Canichers, 1858
Stroud, J. R. G. (late Baudoux & Sons) North Clifton, 1891
Sweetland, William Robert, Vale Road, 1906

Tupper, W. J., Victoria Road, *c*.1811

Valpied, Mrs., 20 Mount Row
Valpied, Peter, Victoria Terrace, 1867

Warner, J., 5 Pollet, 1858 (formerly of Regent Street, London)
Westness, T., 132 Victoria Road (later in Alderney, 1886)
Woodwards, W. J., Havilland Street, *c*.1910

180.   The portrait photographer James Burnside had a studio at 5 Pollet in 1886. The studio was taken over by T. A. Grut in 1894. This is a James Burnside *carte de visite*.

181. A second James Burnside *carte de visite*.

182. A photograph of Mrs. Florence Coysh.

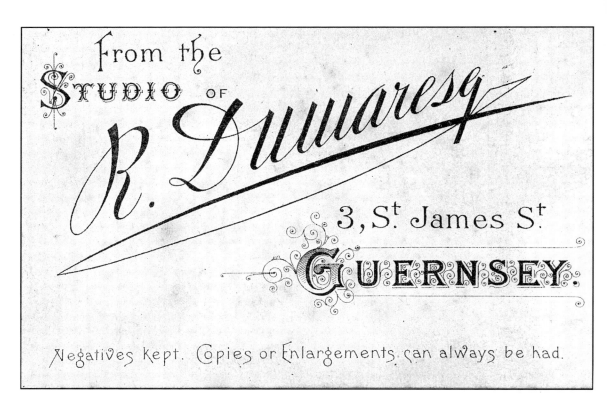

183. An R. Dumaresq *carte de visite* from the turn of the century.

184. Reverse of R. Dumaresq's *carte de visite*.

185. The photographer T. A. Grut worked from 2 Victoria Crescent between 1879 and 1894, when he moved to 5 Pollet.
He was followed by his son, Norman, his grandson, Alan, and his great-grandson, Dave Grut. This photograph shows
the Maunder family: Wilfred, Albert, Arthur James, Clifford, Leonard, Arthur William and Ethel.

186. One of Guernsey's leading professional portrait photographers was John F. Le Quelenec, A.I.I.P., who started work as a boy at Grut's when he was aged 14 and stayed there for 55 years. He died in 1975. In his early days at Grut's lighting was mainly natural and when this failed arc lamps were brought in. Glass plates up to 10 in. by 8 in. were used. Developing was accomplished by rocking the developer over a dishful of plates under a very dim red light. Printing by contact was almost entirely in frames with little enlarging.

187. Billy Rowswell was a well-known island character whose voice could be heard advertising newspapers in the streets of St Peter Port for nearly 75 years. He became a news boy in 1900 and was never able to read or write. He died in 1982 at the age of ninety-one. This studio portrait was taken by John F. Le Quelenec.

188. John (Quill) Bisset was a founder member of the Guernsey Photographic Club in 1953. An amateur photographer of the highest calibre, he served as the club's president for 15 years and worked unceasingly to further the art and pass on his photographic skills to all. He died in 1986.

189. A view of L'Ancresse Bay, by John Bisset.

190. Wilfred New was a St Peter Port street cleaner during the mid-1930s. Norman Grut had this striking silhouette of him accepted by the Professional Photographers' Association for an exhibition at the Royal Institute Galleries, Piccadilly, in 1937.

This amusing cartoon commentary on officials and others at the Grand Havre Regatta in 1 July 1931 was drawn by 'Mac', a local artist whose work was much admired. His drawings often appeared in advertisements in the *Guernsey Evening Press*. The reference to 'Utopia' appertains to the regatta's patron, Walter Martin, who owned the *Royal Hotel* and used the word constantly in his publicity. He owned a house at Grand Havre called 'The Crabpot'.